D1240798

HOMEMADE

GLUTEN-FREE

BREAD MACHINE

Baking Delicious Gluten-Free bread
recipes cookbook: A Step-by-Step
Guide to Making Perfect Loaves Every
Time

Doyle C. Wingo

Table of Contents

INTRODUCTION

Olivia had always enjoyed baking, but when she discovered she had a gluten intolerance, she was disappointed that she could no longer enjoy her favorite activity.

But nevertheless, she soon discovered the gluten-free bread machine. She was determined to find the perfect gluten-free bread recipe, so she embarked on a journey of trial and error.

Olivia finally perfected her gluten-free bread recipe after much experimenting and tweaking, and she now enjoys baking even more than she did before.

A gluten-free bread machine is ideal for anyone who wants to make delicious gluten-free bread without the hassle of traditional baking methods.

This appliance makes making delicious loaves of bread simple while avoiding gluten contamination. It not only provides a quick and efficient way to make bread, but it also allows bread makers to customize the ingredients and flavors of their bread.

A gluten-free bread machine can produce fresh, delicious bread that is tailored to your dietary requirements.

This machine can help you make healthy gluten-free bread. It's a great way to enjoy homemade bread's flavor and texture without worrying about gluten.

The beauty is that these machines are now available in a variety of shapes and sizes, allowing you to find one that fits your lifestyle and budget. It can help you easily create delicious gluten-free bread with minimal effort, whether you are a beginner or an experienced baker.

With a little knowledge, the chemistry behind the gluten-free bread machine is simple to grasp.

The machine works by first mixing the ingredients in a large mixing bowl, then kneading the dough until thoroughly combined. The dough is then placed in a loaf pan, and the machine does the rest.

This method ensures that the bread is gluten-free and allows you to tailor the ingredients and flavors to your desires.

CHAPTER 1

Bread Machine Basics

Bread machine home baking is a simple and convenient way to make delicious, homemade bread.

You can create delicious, homemade loaves of bread, rolls, and other baked goods with just a few ingredients, a bread machine, and minimal effort.

Bread machine baking at home is simple. Most bread machines have different settings for different types of bread, such as white, whole wheat, and rye.

The bread machine does the rest after you select the settings and begin the baking process. It makes the bread for you by mixing, kneading, and baking it.

It is, in fact, very premium.

A basic bread machine can be purchased for as little as $50 and can produce a wide range of delicious slices of bread, rolls, and other baked goods. Use less expensive ingredients like whole wheat flour, oats, and honey to save money.

The machine is also highly adaptable. You can play around with different ingredients and flavors to make a one-of-a-kind, delicious loaf of bread.

Bread machine baking also allows you to make a variety of shapes, sizes, and textures, making it a fun way to experiment in the kitchen.

Overall, bread machine home baking is an excellent way to create delicious, homemade bread, rolls, and other baked goods with little effort and expense. It's a quick, inexpensive, and versatile way to enjoy the flavor of fresh bread.

Bread Maker

A bread maker is a kitchen appliance used to bake bread. It typically consists of a bread pan or bucket, a heating element, and a timer. The user adds all the ingredients to the bread pan, sets the timer, and the machine automatically mixes, kneads, and bakes the bread.

Bread Maker Categories

1. Programmable Bread Maker: A tunable bread maker is a machine used to make bread. It has several features that allow the user to personalize their bread-making experience.

A bread maker typically includes a bread pan in which to place the ingredients, a timer to determine how long the bread should bake, and a variety of settings to adjust for the type of bread being made.

The user can choose from multiple bread settings, including whole wheat, white, French, and rapid. After selecting the type of bread, the user can adjust the settings to account for the number of ingredients used, the amount of time the bread needs to be baked, and the temperature of the oven.

According to the user's settings, the bread maker will automatically mix the ingredients, knead the dough, and bake the bread.

After the bread has finished baking, the user can remove it from the pan and enjoy their freshly baked bread.

The programmable bread maker is an excellent tool for those who enjoy experimenting with various types of bread and customizing their bread-making experience.

2. Manual Bread Maker: A manual bread maker is a kitchen appliance that lets you make bread without using electricity.

The bread maker is more than just a machine that bakes bread.

Do you recall how your house smelled when you got home from school and your mother was baking bread for dinner? Aside from the fresh smell of laundry drying outside, one of my most nostalgic memories is the smell of bread baking in the kitchen.

Even though we would like to, it is difficult to bake fresh bread every day due to our hectic schedules. Making the dough, kneading, waiting for it to rise twice, and then baking it takes more time than any of us can devote.

The introduction of the bread machine, on the other hand, has simplified the task. Now you can put your ingredients in the machine's container, set it according to the instructions, and the machine will knead the dough and bake a loaf for you.

If you get a machine with a timer, it will turn off when the loaf is done, and the aroma of fresh bread will fill the house, greeting you at the door side when you get home from work.

You can use your machine for purposes other than baking bread. In most cases, the machine has a feature that allows you to only make the dough. That dough can then be used to make rolls, coffee cakes, pizza dough, or whatever else you can think of. Homemade bread is comfort food for many people, and it starts with the aroma of freshly baked bread permeating the entire house.

If you don't have a bread machine, we recommend purchasing one and beginning to create some nostalgic memories for your family.

A bread-making machine can make white bread, rye bread, onion bread, wheat bread, French bread, and many other types of bread.

Your bread machine will come with an instruction manual and recipes for various types of bread. The manual is where the fun begins, as it allows you to experiment with different types of bread.

To purchase a bread machine, decide where you want to put it in your kitchen and then look for a machine that will fit into that space. You should also calculate how much bread your family consumes and buy the appropriate size to avoid wasting bread.

If you make too much bread, you can always dry it and make homemade breadcrumbs, which are far superior to store-bought breadcrumbs.

This appliance has numerous advantages, which include:

• Quick Processing: It is not necessary to be present while the bread is baking. Even bread machines can be programmed to bake fresh bread when you finish your work.

• Versatility: In addition to bread, the device can bake crusts, baguettes, rolls, and fresh pizza bases.

• Steam: With advanced models, steam can be used to bake bread. It enables the consumption of softer and healthier bread.

• Minimal manual intervention: Due to the advanced model's pre-programmed programming, you only need to put all of the ingredients into it and turn it on.

• Healthy bread: This bread made at home is healthier because it does not contain any preservatives found in store-bought bread.

This device is quickly becoming a small appliance that is almost as widely used as the microwave oven. These machines are kitchen miracles that will make our cooking and baking lives easier.

3. Automatic Bread Maker: A bread machine is a kitchen appliance that automates the bread-making process. It usually consists of a container with a heating element and a timer at the bottom.

The user places the ingredients in the container (flour, water, yeast, salt, etc.), sets the timer, and the machine does the rest.

The machine kneads the dough, mixes the ingredients, and bakes the bread. When the baking process is finished, the device automatically turns off.

Automatic breadmakers are extremely popular these days. The bread you can make smells and tastes fantastic, and making your own homemade bread is extremely simple nowadays. Forget about being afraid of hard work or having your kitchen look like your children went on a rampage in it. You can no longer go wrong with an automated bread maker.

But what should you look for when deciding which one is right for you? Let me explain a few things, some obvious, some not so obvious. It should give you a good idea of what to think about before you buy.

The primary benefits of using an automatic bread machine are convenience and time savings. The user does not have to constantly monitor the bread-making process because the machine does most of the work. Furthermore, bread ranging from traditional white bread to specialty bread can be made.

The user can adjust the baking time, the color of the crust, and other settings to their liking.

4. Gluten-Free Bread Maker: A Gluten-Free Bread Maker is a kitchen appliance that is specifically designed to bake gluten-free bread.

The appliance can be used to make gluten-free cakes, cookies, muffins, and pizza dough. Gluten-free bread makers are becoming increasingly popular as the number of people who are gluten intolerant and want to reduce their gluten intake grows.

If you've ever tried to find gluten-free bread, you'll know that it's not easy to buy, and even if you do, it can be quite expensive. The other issue is that once you've paid for your overpriced loaf, you'd rather use it as a doorstop or a paperweight than eat it. If this is the case for you, another option is to create your own.

Making your own gluten-free bread can be difficult if you have never done it before, but with the right recipe and technique, you can make an excellent loaf of bread with great flavor and texture that can be used for sandwiches, toast, French toast, or even eaten plain.

Using a Gluten-Free Bread Maker is simple and straightforward. Simply add your ingredients, select a program, and let the machine do the rest. The appliance will mix, knead, rise, and bake your gluten-free bread to perfection.

Most machines come with pre-programmed programs that allow you to quickly create a variety of different products. Many models also have delayed start options, allowing you to program the machine to begin baking later.

Gluten is the elastic protein found in wheat, rye, and barley that gives bread its elasticity and ability to rise high, resulting in a nice, fluffy loaf.

However, with a good recipe, proper technique, and possibly the assistance of a quality bread machine, you can make your own gluten-free bread that is quite tasty and quite easy to make.

Gluten-Free Flours and Starches

Almond Flour

Almond flour is a gluten-free, nutritious flour made from finely ground almonds. It is high in healthy fats, protein, fiber, vitamins, and minerals, making it an ideal gluten-free or wheat-free alternative to traditional wheat flour. It also has a mild, nutty flavor that can be used to complement a variety of recipes.

Health Benefits

1. High in Nutrients: Almond flour contains a variety of essential nutrients such as vitamin E, copper, magnesium, and manganese.

2. High in Healthy Fats: Almond flour contains a lot of healthy unsaturated fats, which can help lower bad cholesterol and improve heart health.

3. Low in Carbs: Almond flour is low in carbs, making it an excellent low-carb option.

4. Gluten-Free: Almond flour is naturally gluten-free, making it an excellent choice for those who are sensitive to or allergic to gluten.

5. High in Fiber: Almond flour contains a lot of fiber, which is good for digestion and gut health.

How to Get the Best Out of Almond Flour

1. Use it in place of wheat flour: Almond flour can be used in place of wheat flour in many recipes. However, because it does not rise like wheat flour, it is best used in recipes that do not require rinsing.

2. Add it to smoothies: Almond flour is an excellent way to boost your smoothies' protein and fiber content.

3. Use it in baking: Almond flour can be used in a variety of baking recipes, including cookies, muffins, and bread.

4. Prepare almond meal: Grind almonds into coarse flour to make an almond meal. It can be substituted for almond flour in a variety of recipes.

5. Use it to thicken sauces and gravies: Almond flour can be used to thicken sauces and gravies.

6. Pancakes: Gluten-free pancakes can be made with almond flour.

7. Replace breadcrumbs with almond flour: Instead of breadcrumbs, almond flour can be used to coat chicken, fish, or vegetables.

8. Prepare almond milk: Almond flour can be used to make delicious and nutritious almond milk.

9. Make energy bars: Delicious energy bars can be made with almond flour.

10. Make almond butter with almond flour: Almond flour can be used to make homemade almond butter.

11. Add it to oatmeal: Almond flour can be mixed into oatmeal to add a nutty flavor.

12. Use it in desserts: Almond flour can be used to make a wide range of delectable desserts, including cakes, pies, and cookies.

13. Use it in granola: Almond flour can be used in granola to add a crunchy texture.

14. Use it as a binding agent in veggie burgers: Almond flour can be used as a binding agent in veggie burgers.

15. Make gluten-free pasta with almond flour: Almond flour can be used to make gluten-free pasta.

Coconut Flour

Coconut flour is a healthy, low-carb alternative to other grain-based flour. It is made from dried and ground mature coconut flesh.

Health Benefits of Coconut Flour:

1. High in fiber: With 5 grams of fiber per two-tablespoon plateful, coconut flour is an excellent source of dietary fiber. Dietary fiber aids digestion improves gut health and promotes satiety after meals.

2. Gluten-free: Because coconut flour is naturally gluten-free, it is an ideal choice for gluten-free people.

3. Low in carbohydrates: Because coconut flour contains fewer carbohydrates than other types of flour, it is a great replacement for those on a low-carb diet.

4. High in healthy fats: Coconut flour contains a lot of healthy fats, like medium-chain triglycerides (MCTs), which have been linked to a variety of health benefits.

5. High in protein: Coconut flour contains 5 grams of plant-based protein per two tablespoon serving.

6. Low in sugar: Because coconut flour is naturally low in sugar, it is an excellent choice for those on a low-sugar diet.

How to get the best out of Coconut Flour:

1. Combine coconut flour and other flours: While coconut flour can be used alone, combining it with other flours often results in a lighter texture. Try combining coconut flour with almond flour or oat flour for baked goods.

2. Add more liquid: Because coconut flour absorbs a lot of liquid, it's important to add more liquid when using it in recipes. Begin with 1/4 cup more liquid than called for in the recipe and adjust as needed.

3. Add an additional binding agent: To keep the dough together, coconut flour frequently requires the addition of additional binding agents such as eggs or flaxseed meals.

4. Bake at a lower temperature: Because coconut flour bakes at a lower temperature than other flours, reduce the temperature accordingly.

5. Bake in smaller pans: Because coconut flour produces a denser texture, bake in smaller pans when using it.

6. Sift the coconut flour: Because coconut flour can be clumpy, sift it before adding it to the other ingredients.

Arrowroot Flour

Arrowroot flour is a flexible and gluten-free substitute for wheat flour. It has several health benefits, including being high in dietary fiber, essential vitamins, and minerals and low in calories.

Health Benefits:

1. High in Dietary Fiber: Arrowroot flour contains a lot of dietary fiber, which is good for digestion and regular bowel movements.

2. Low in Calories: Because arrowroot flour is low in calories, it is an excellent choice for those attempting to lose or maintain a healthy weight.

3. Contains Essential Vitamins and Minerals: Arrowroot flour contains essential vitamins and minerals such as magnesium, zinc, iron, and calcium.

4. Gluten-Free: Because arrowroot flour is naturally gluten-free, it is an excellent choice for people who have celiac disease or gluten sensitivities.

5. Low Glycemic Index: Because arrowroot flour has a low glycemic index, it will not cause a rapid drop in blood sugar when consumed.

How to Get the Best Out of Arrowroot Flour:

1. Wheat Flour Substitute: Arrowroot flour can be used in place of wheat flour in many recipes.

2. Add to Smoothies: For added fiber and nutrition, add a tablespoon of arrowroot flour to your smoothie.

3. Use It in Baking: Arrowroot flour can be used in recipes for cakes, muffins, cookies, and other baked goods.

4. Thicken Sauces and Soups: Arrowroot flour works well as a thickener in soups and sauces.

5. Make Pancakes: For a gluten-free and nutritious breakfast, try making pancakes with arrowroot flour.

Arrowroot flour can also be used to bind ingredients together, such as in meatballs or veggie burgers.

7. Make Gluten-Free Pasta: You can make gluten-free pasta with arrowroot flour.

8. Make Gluten-Free Bread: To make gluten-free bread and rolls, use arrowroot flour.

9. Use as a Coating: Arrowroot flour can also be used to coat meats and vegetables before frying or baking.

10. Make Gluten-Free Crackers: To make gluten-free crackers and chips, use arrowroot flour.

11. As a Batter: Arrowroot flour makes an excellent batter for fried foods.

12. Make a Gluten-Free Pizza Crust: Arrowroot flour can be used to make a tasty gluten-free pizza crust.

Teff Flour

Teff flour is a high-nutrient flour made from the ancient grain of teff. It is high in fiber, calcium, iron, and a variety of other vitamins and minerals. It is also gluten-free and low in calories, making it a wonderful replacement for wheat flour in baked goods. Teff flour is an excellent way to boost the nutritional value of any recipe.

Health Advantages:

1. High in Fiber: Teff flour is high in fiber, which can help support digestive health and keep you fuller for longer.

2. High in iron: Teff flour is high in iron, which is required for healthy red blood cells.

3. Calcium-Rich: Teff flour is high in calcium, which is essential for bone health and muscle function.

4. Gluten-free: Teff flour is gluten-free, making it an excellent choice for those who must avoid gluten in their diet.

5. Low in Calories: Teff flour is very low in calories, making it an excellent choice for those watching their calorie intake.

How to Make the Most of Teff Flour:

1. Substitute for Other Flours: In most recipes, teff flour can be used in place of wheat flour. It can be

used to make pancakes, waffles, bread, muffins, cookies, and other baked goods.

2. Use in Smoothies: Teff flour can be added to smoothies to provide a nutritious and filling start to the day.

3. Use Teff Flour to Thicken Soups and Sauces: Teff flour can be used to thicken soups and sauces. It also improves the nutritional value of dishes.

4. Use as a Gluten-Free Breadcrumb Substitute: Teff flour can be used as a gluten-free breadcrumb substitute in recipes.

5. Thickener: Teff flour can be used to thicken sauces, soups, and stews.

By following these guidelines, you can maximize the nutritional value of teff flour.

Rice Flour

Rice flour is a gluten-free alternative to wheat flour, making it an ideal choice for those suffering from celiac disease or gluten intolerance. It also has more fiber and fewer calories than wheat flour. Rice flour is high in vitamins and minerals such as niacin, thiamin, phosphorus, and potassium.

Health Privileges:

1. Gluten-Free: Rice flour is a great gluten-free alternative to wheat flour if you are gluten intolerant or have celiac disease.

2. High in Fiber: Rice flour contains more fiber than wheat flour and thus provides more nutrients to the diet.

3. Lower in Calories: Rice flour has fewer calories than wheat flour, making it a healthier option for dieters.

4. High in Vitamins and Minerals: Rice flour is high in vitamins and minerals such as niacin, thiamin, phosphorus, and potassium.

How to Make the Most of Rice Flour:

1. Use it as a Thickening Agent: Rice flour can be used to thicken soups and sauces.

2. Make Gluten-Free Baked Goods with It: Rice flour can be used to make delicious gluten-free baked goods like cakes, muffins, and cookies.

3. Make Pancakes: Rice flour can be used to make light and fluffy pancakes.

4. Bread: Rice flour can be combined with other gluten-free flour, such as tapioca flour, to make gluten-free bread.

5. Make Noodles with It: Rice flour can also be used to make gluten-free noodles.

6. Make Porridge with it: Rice flour can also be used to make porridge.

7. Use it as a Coating: Before frying or baking, coat meat and vegetables with rice flour.

8. Use it as a Binder: Rice flour can be used to make meatloaf or burger patties.

9. Breading: Rice flour can be used as breading for fried foods.

10. Make gluten-free wraps with it: Rice flour can also be used to make gluten-free wraps.

Sweet Rice Flour

Sweet Rice Flour is a nutritious, gluten-free flour with therapeutic properties. It is low in calories and fat, high in minerals, and high in vitamins and nutrients.

Health Benefits:

1. Sweet rice flour is a high-energy food. It is a complex carbohydrate with slow-release energy that keeps you fuller for longer.

2. Sweet rice flour contains a lot of fiber, which aids digestion and keeps you feeling fuller for longer.

3. Sweet rice flour is also high in vitamins and minerals such as B vitamins, iron, magnesium, and zinc.

4. Sweet rice flour is low in fat and cholesterol, making it a healthier option than other flour.

5. Sweet rice flour is gluten-free, which is advantageous for those suffering from celiac disease or gluten intolerance.

How to Make the Most of Sweet Rice Flour:

1. Use sweet rice flour in place of other flour in baking. It's ideal for baking cakes, brownies, muffins, and other baked goods.

2. Sweet rice flour can be used to thicken sauces and gravies.

3. Make gluten-free pancakes and waffles with sweet rice flour.

4. Make gluten-free pizza crusts with sweet rice flour.

5. Coat chicken, fish, and other proteins in sweet rice flour before pan-frying.

6. Make gluten-free bread and rolls with sweet rice flour.

7. Use sweet rice flour instead of regular flour in Asian dishes like dumplings and noodles.

8. Make gluten-free desserts like cookies, bars, and pies with sweet rice flour.

9. Make a delicious gluten-free porridge or congee with sweet rice flour.

10. Make gluten-free pasta with sweet rice flour.

Potato Flour & Potato Starch

Potato flour and potato starch are both highly nutritious potato recipes.

Whole potatoes are cooked, dried, and ground into a fine flour to make potato flour. It contains a lot of carbohydrates, fiber, vitamins, and minerals. Potato flour is gluten-free and can be used in place of wheat flour.

Potato starch is made by grinding peeled, cooked, and dried potatoes into a fine powder. It is high in complex carbohydrates and is used in cooking as a thickening agent. Potato starch is also gluten-free and can be used in baking recipes in place of all-purpose flour.

Health Advantages:

Potato flour and potato starch are both high in complex carbohydrates and dietary fiber, which may aid in blood sugar regulation and digestion. They are also naturally gluten-free, making them an excellent choice for people suffering from Celiac disease or gluten sensitivity.

Both potato flour and potato starch are high in vitamins and minerals like iron, magnesium, phosphorus, and zinc. They are also high in B vitamins necessary for energy production and metabolism.

Making the Most of Potato Flour and Potato Starch:

It is important to note that potato flour and potato starch absorb more liquid than wheat flour, so recipes may require more liquid to achieve the desired consistency.

Potato starch and flour can be used to thicken sauces, soups, and gravies. They can also be used in place of all-purpose flour when baking.

Use half the amount of Potato Flour or Potato Starch as the amount of all-purpose flour called for in the recipe when substituting.

Potato Flour and Potato Starch can be combined with other gluten-free flour in baking to create a more nutritious and flavorful baked product.

It is best to consult a qualified health professional or nutritionist for even more information on recipes and uses for potato flour and potato starch.

Tapioca Starch

Tapioca starch is a gluten-free, natural starch obtained from cassava root. It's a white powdery substance used to thicken sauces and desserts. It's also a popular gluten-free baking ingredient. Tapioca starch is high in carbohydrates, low in fat and protein, and packed with vitamins and minerals.

Health Advantages:

1. High in Vitamins and Minerals: Tapioca starch is high in a variety of vitamins and minerals. It is high in calcium, phosphorus, magnesium, folate, and B vitamins, all of which are necessary for bone health and energy levels.

2. High in Fiber: Tapioca starch is high in dietary fiber, which promotes digestive health and keeps you feeling fuller for longer.

3. Gluten-Free: Tapioca starch is gluten-free, making it an excellent substitute for wheat-based flour for those who have gluten sensitivities or intolerances.

4. Low-Calorie: Tapioca starch has a low-calorie count, making it an excellent choice for those attempting to lose or maintain weight.

How to Make the Most of Tapioca Starch:

1. Thickening Agent: Tapioca starch is an excellent thickening agent for sauces and gravies. To use it as a thickener, combine a small amount of starch with cold water or another liquid before adding it to the recipe.

2. Use it in Baking: Tapioca starch can be used in baking in place of wheat flour. It has a light and fluffy texture and can aid in the binding of ingredients.

3. Use it to thicken soups and stews: Tapioca starch can thicken soups and stews. It will thicken as it cools, so add it at the end of the cooking time.

4. Egg Substitute: Tapioca starch can be used in vegan recipes as an egg substitute. Simply combine 1 tablespoon of starch and 1 tablespoon of water for each egg required in the recipe.

5. Create a Gluten-Free Pie Crust: Tapioca starch can be used to create a gluten-free pie crust. Combine 1 cup tapioca starch, 1/4 cup nondairy milk, 1/4 cup melted coconut oil, and 1/4 teaspoon salt in a mixing bowl. Form a dough and press it into a pie plate.

Make Gluten-Free Pancakes: Tapioca starch can be used to make gluten-free pancakes. Simply combine 1 cup tapioca starch, 1 cup almond milk, 1 tablespoon melted coconut oil, and 1 teaspoon baking powder in a mixing bowl. Cook on a hot griddle until a batter forms.

7. Create a Creamy Pudding: Tapioca starch can be used to make a creamy pudding. Simply combine

1/2 cup tapioca starch, 1/2 cup nondairy milk, 1/4 cup melted coconut oil, 1/4 cup maple syrup, and 1 teaspoon vanilla extract in a mixing bowl. Cook until thickened over medium heat.

Tapioca starch can be used to make the popular tapioca pearls. Simply mix 1 cup tapioca starch and 1 cup boiling water. Roll into small balls after forming a dough. Boil for 15 minutes in water and serve.

9. Tapioca starch can be used to make fried rice. Simply combine the starch with the cooked rice and fry until golden brown.

10. Tapioca starch can be used to make gluten-free pasta. Combine 1/2 cup tapioca starch, 1/2 cup nondairy milk, 1/4 cup melted coconut oil, and 1/2 teaspoon salt in a mixing bowl. Roll the dough out and cut it into the desired shapes. Cook until al dente in boiling water.

Sorghum Flour

Sorghum flour is a gluten-free, nutritious flour produced by grinding the entire grain of sorghum. It is high in fiber, protein, and minerals and is an ideal option for wheat flour. It is suitable for making pancakes, muffins, cakes, and other baked goods.

Health Benefits:

1. Sorghum flour is high in dietary fiber, which can help you feel full and lower your cholesterol levels.

2. It contains minerals such as iron, magnesium, and zinc, which can benefit your overall health.

3. Sorghum flour is a gluten-free alternative to wheat flour, making it an excellent choice for those suffering from celiac disease or gluten sensitivity.

4. It is a good source of protein, which can aid in the development and maintenance of muscle mass.

How to Make the Most of Sorghum Flour:

1. Begin by replacing a small amount of wheat flour in your recipes with sorghum flour. Begin with

a 1:2 or 1:3 ratio and gradually increase the amount of sorghum flour until you achieve the desired taste and texture.

2. If you use sorghum flour instead of wheat flour, you may need to add more liquid to your recipes. Begin with a 1/2 cup of extra liquid for every cup of sorghum flour.

3. Sorghum flour works best when combined with a gluten-free flour such as almond flour, coconut flour, and oat flour.

4. To ensure that your baked goods rise properly, add a teaspoon of baking powder for every cup of sorghum flour used.

5. Allow enough time for your dough or batter to rest before baking with sorghum flour. This will ensure that your baked goods are light and fluffy.

6. For added nutrition and texture, add a tablespoon of ground flaxseed or chia seed to your recipes.

Millet Flour

Millet flour is high in nutrients and can be beneficial to your well-being. It is a whole-grain flour high in fiber, B vitamins, phosphorus, magnesium, and manganese. It is also low in calories, fat, and sodium, making it a nutritious addition to any diet.

Millet Flour Health Benefits:

1. Improves Heart Health: Millet flour contains magnesium, which can help lower blood pressure and the risk of heart disease.

2. Promotes Digestive Health: Millet flour is high in dietary fiber, which aids in regularity and the prevention of constipation.

3. Improves Blood Sugar Control: Because millet flour has a low glycemic index, it can help regulate blood sugar levels.

4. Aids in Weight Loss: Millet flour is low in calories and fat, making it an excellent addition to any diet.

5. Promotes Bone Health: Millet flour contains phosphorus, which is necessary for strong bones and teeth.

Making the Most out of Millet Flour:

1. Bake with it: Millet flour can be used in a variety of baked goods, from muffins to bread.

2. Add to soups and sauces: Millet flour can be used to thicken and add nutrition to soups and sauces.

3. Use it as a coating: Before baking or frying, coat foods like chicken or fish with millet flour.

4. Make a porridge out of it: Millet flour can be used to make a tasty and nutritious porridge.

5. Add to smoothies: Blend millet flour into smoothies for a nutritious and filling snack or meal.

With so many health benefits and versatility, millet flour is an ideal choice for a healthy lifestyle.

Quinoa Flour

Quinoa flour is a gluten-free and nutritious alternative to wheat flour, with various health benefits. It is high in protein and fiber, and it contains a variety of vitamins and minerals. Quinoa flour can be used in a diverse variety of recipes, including bread, desserts, and savory dishes.

Health Advantages:

- Quinoa flour has a high protein content and contains all nine essential amino acids.
- It's also high in dietary fiber, which can help with digestion.
- Quinoa flour is gluten-free, making it an excellent choice for those suffering from celiac disease or gluten sensitivity.

- Quinoa flour contains a variety of vitamins and minerals, including B vitamins, magnesium, iron, and potassium.
- Quinoa flour is also high in antioxidants, which can prevent inflammation and disease.

How to Make the Most of Quinoa Flour:

- Quinoa flour, which has a slightly nutty flavor, is a great alternative to wheat flour in baking recipes.

• Quinoa flour can be combined with other flours to make a healthier, more nutrient-dense baked good.

• Quinoa flour can also be used to thicken soups and sauces instead of wheat flour or cornstarch.

• Quinoa flour can be used in savory dishes like pancakes, muffins, and bread.

• Quinoa flour is also a good choice for coating food before frying because it contributes to a crispy texture.

• Quinoa flour can be stored in an airtight container in a cool, dry place for up to six months.

• Quinoa flour can be used in a wide range of recipes, such as desserts, pancakes, cookies, muffins, and bread.

• Quinoa flour can also be used in savory dishes like dumplings, wontons, and crusts in place of wheat flour.

Brown Rice Flour

Brown rice flour is a healthy and tasty option for white flour. It is high in fiber, protein, and essential vitamins and minerals like iron, magnesium, and B. It also contains lignans, which are anti-inflammatory and antioxidant in nature. Brown rice flour also has a lower glycemic index than white flour, making it a better choice for those who suffer from diabetes or other metabolic disorders.

How to Make the Most of Brown Rice Flour:

• Retain it in a cool, dry location. When exposed to high temperatures or humidity, brown rice flour can go rancid.

• Use it in recipes as a partial replacement. Brown rice flour can be used to replace up to half of the white flour in a recipe. This will give your finished product a nutty flavor and more nutrition.

• Combine it with other gluten-free flour. Brown rice flour can be quite dense on its own, so it is best combined with other gluten-free flour such as almond flour or coconut flour.

• Incorporate ground flaxseed or chia into your recipes. These seeds will increase your final product's fiber, protein, and B vitamins.

• Experiment with various recipes. Pancakes, waffles, muffins, cakes, and even pizza crusts can be made with brown rice flour. Have some fun and get creative.

Buckwheat Flour

Buckwheat flour is a gluten-free, nutritious alternative to traditional wheat flour that is high in fiber, protein, vitamins, and minerals. It contains a lot of antioxidants, which can help reduce inflammation and protect you from diseases like cancer and heart disease. Buckwheat flour can also aid in cholesterol reduction and blood sugar regulation.

How to Make the Most of Buckwheat Flour:

• Use it in place of wheat flour in recipes. Buckwheat flour can be used in place of wheat flour in a variety of recipes, including pancakes, muffins, bread, and cakes.

• Combine it with other types of flour. Buckwheat flour has a distinct, nutty flavor and can be combined with other flours such as rice, oat, and almond to produce distinctive baked goods.

• Include it in smoothies and shakes. Buckwheat flour can be used to boost the nutritional value of smoothies and shakes while also adding a nutty flavor.

• It can be used to thicken sauces. Without adding gluten, buckwheat flour can thicken sauces, gravies, and soups.

Gluten-free flour and starches can be an ideal option for wheat-based products for those who are gluten intolerant or have Celiac disease. They are also an excellent choice for those looking to reduce their intake of wheat.

Gluten-free flour and starches can be used to make a variety of delicious dishes, with possible choices such as almond flour, tapioca starch, and rice flour. It is critical to remember to carefully read the labels to ensure that the products are gluten-free.

Gluten-Free Yeast

Yeast is required for several life processes, including digestion and the production of various food products such as bread and beer. Because of these functions, bacteria are present in the body and, in general, do not cause much harm.

However, some people are extremely sensitive to yeast and have severe reactions, so understanding these reactions is critical in determining whether you or a family member has a yeast allergy.

Symptoms of Yeast Allergy

Because yeast allergy symptoms are so diverse, it can be difficult to determine the true cause of some of them. Sore throat, sneezing, headache, and congestion are mild reaction symptoms, while skin rash, diarrhea, constipation, vomiting, and abdominal pain are more severe. Most, if not all, of these symptoms, can be difficult to identify because they are shared by so many other conditions, but a doctor can easily diagnose gluten intolerance in a family member.

Maintaining a Yeast Allergy

Because yeast is used in so many different foods, eliminating it completely from your diet can be difficult. Most bread is made with yeast, but there are gluten-free varieties available for people who are allergic to yeast.

Even in mild cases of yeast allergy, eliminating yeast from your diet is advised because aggravating your condition will cause it to worsen.

When shopping, look for gluten-free items that are specifically labeled. This means they were made without yeast, making them safe to eat. You can also substitute foods in places where you might have eaten yeast products.

Instead of a sandwich for lunch, make some pasta. Pasta contains no yeast or gluten, making it a viable substitute for bread in many situations.

Active Dry Yeast

Active dry yeast is a type of dry yeast that is commonly used in baking and brewing. Saccharomyces cerevisiae is a single-celled organism that is grown on a nutrient-rich medium before being dried and milled into a powder. Active dry yeast has a higher shelf life than fresh yeast, allowing it to be stored for longer periods of time.

Active dry yeast is used to leaven bread doughs, giving them the necessary lift and structure for a good loaf of bread. The yeast in the ingredients converts the sugar in the ingredients into alcohol and carbon dioxide, causing the dough or liquid to rise and become light and fluffy.

Active dry yeast is sold in packets or jars and should be kept cool and dry. It should be rehydrated in warm water before use to bring it back to life.

When baking, it is critical to use the correct amount of yeast, as too much can cause the dough to rise too quickly and become overly yeasty. A dense, heavy loaf will result from using too little yeast.

Instant Yeast

Instant yeast, also known as rapid-rise yeast, quick-rise yeast, fast-rising yeast, or bread machine yeast, is a baking yeast. This baking yeast is created by combining active dry yeast and a type of instant yeast. It is more resistant to temperature changes and rises faster than active dry yeast.

As a result, it is ideal for recipes requiring a quick rise time, such as bread, rolls, and pizza dough. Instant yeast is also a good option for bread machine recipes because it can be added directly to the ingredients without being proofed or dissolved in water.

Instant yeast, unlike active dry yeast, does not need to be "proofed" or dissolved in water before use. This makes using it in recipes much easier and faster.

It is also more convenient for bakers because it has a longer shelf life than active dry yeast.

Instant yeast is best used in recipes that do not require a long rising period due to its faster rise time. It's not as good for recipes that call for a slow rise, like sourdough bread. It is best to use active dry yeast in these recipes.

When replacing active dry yeast with instant yeast, use half the amount specified in the recipe. If a recipe calls for 2 teaspoons of active dry yeast, substitute 1 teaspoon of instant yeast.

It is best to keep instant yeast in a cool, dry place when storing it. It does not need to be refrigerated, but it can be kept in the freezer for up to a year.

Instant yeast is ideal for recipes that require a quick rise time. It is simpler to use and lasts longer than active dry yeast. It is not, however, a good choice for recipes that call for a slow rise.

Rapid Rise Yeast

Rapid Rise Yeast is an active dry yeast that has been specially designed to work quickly and efficiently. It is a type of instant yeast that rises quickly and gives the dough a light, airy texture. Because it eliminates the need for a long rising time, this yeast is ideal for breadmakers who are short on time.

It also removes the need for a proofing and kneading cycle, which makes it easier to work with. Rapid Rise Yeast is ideal for recipes that require a light and fluffy texture, such as focaccia, quick bread, and dinner rolls.

It is great for pizza dough because it eliminates the need for a long rising time, which is especially important when time is limited. Rapid Rise Yeast is also ideal for novice bakers because it eliminates the need for advanced baking techniques. This yeast is available in both regular and quick-rise forms. The quick-rise yeast is designed to rise twice as fast as regular active dry yeast, making it ideal for recipes that call for a quick rise time. It is ideal for time-pressed bread makers, as it eliminates the need for a lengthy proofing and kneading cycle.

It is important to note that Rapid Rise Yeast should not be used for recipes that require a long rising time, as the results will be different.

When using Rapid Rise Yeast, it is critical to carefully follow the instructions and use the yeast before the expiration date. It is also critical to keep the yeast in a cool, dry place away from moisture and humidity.

This yeast is an excellent choice for those looking for a quick and simple way to make delicious bread and other baked goods.

CHAPTER 2

Bread Maker Recipes

Simple White Bread

Ingredients:

-3 cups all-purpose flour

-2 tablespoons sugar

-1 teaspoon salt

-2 1/4 teaspoons active dry yeast

-1 1/3 cups water

-2 tablespoons vegetable oil

Instructions:

1. In the order listed, add the flour, salt, sugar, and oil to the bread machine pan.

2. Sprinkle the yeast on top, making sure it does not encounter the wet ingredients.

3. Saturate the pan up halfway with warm water.

4. Close the bread machine lid and select the white bread setting.

5. Turn on the machine.

6. When the cycle is complete, take the dough out of the machine.

7. Knead the dough for 5 minutes on a lightly floured surface, or until it is smooth and elastic.

8. Roll the dough into a ball and place it on a greased baking sheet.

9. Cover the dough with a clean cloth and set aside for about an hour, or until doubled in size.

10. Bake for 15-20 minutes, or until the loaf is golden brown, at 375°F.

11. Remove the bread from the oven and set it aside to cool before slicing and eating.

Rye Bread Leftovers

Ingredients:

-1 1/2 cups water

-2 tablespoons olive oil

-2 tablespoons honey

-2 teaspoons salt

-2 1/2 cups bread flour

-1/2 cup rye flour

-2 teaspoons active dry yeast

Instructions:

1. In a large mixing bowl, whisk together the bread flour, all-purpose flour, yeast, salt, and caraway seeds until equally combined.

2. Combine the molasses, water, and vegetable oil in a separate bowl.

3. Combine the wet and dry ingredients and stir until the dough is smooth and elastic.

4. Shape the dough into a ball and set it aside in a lightly oiled bowl. Place the bowl in the refrigerator overnight, covered with plastic wrap.

5. Remove the dough the next morning and knead in the rye flour on a lightly floured surface.

6. Return the dough to the bowl and let it rise in a warm place for one hour, or until it has doubled in size.

7. After the dough has risen, divide it into two round loaves. Place the loaves on a greased baking sheet and allow them to rise for an additional hour.

8. Preheat the oven to 350 degrees Fahrenheit (175 degrees Celsius). Bake for about 30 minutes, or until golden brown.

9. Remove from oven and set aside to cool before slicing.

Focaccia with Herbs

Ingredients

-3 cups all-purpose flour

-1 packet rapid-rise yeast

-1 teaspoon of sugar

-2 teaspoons of dried oregano

-1 pinch of salt

-2 tablespoons of olive oil

-2 tablespoons of fresh rosemary, minced.

-1/2 cup warm water

-1/2 cup of warm whole milk

Instructions

1. Whisk together the flour, yeast, sugar, oregano, and salt in a large mixing bowl. Mix until well combined.

2. Make a well in the center of the mixture and add the olive oil, rosemary, warm water, and warm milk.

3. Using a spoon, combine the ingredients to form a dough.

4. Turn the dough out onto a lightly floured surface and knead for 5 minutes, or until it becomes smooth and elastic.

5. Place the dough in a lightly floured bowl and cover it with a damp cloth or plastic wrap for about an hour.

6. When the dough is ready, place it in the preheated Herb Focaccia Bread machine's greased pan.

7. Bake according to the machine's instructions. Remove the bread from the pan and serve warm or cold.

Cinnamon Roll Dough for a Bread Machine

Ingredients:

-2 cups all-purpose flour

-3/4 cups whole milk

-1/3 cup white sugar

-1 teaspoon salt

-2 1/4 teaspoons active dry yeast

-1/4 cup butter, melted.

-1/2 teaspoon ground cinnamon

Instructions:

1. Add the flour and dry active yeast to the bread machine's baking pan.

2. In a separate bowl, combine the milk, sugar, and salt, stirring until the sugar has dissolved.

3. Pour the milk mixture and melted butter into the baking pan with the flour and yeast, stirring until the ingredients are combined.

4. Add the ground cinnamon, stirring until all is blended.

5. Place the baking pan into the bread machine, closing the lid.

6. Select the "dough" setting and press "start."

7. The dough will rise twice before it is complete, about 45 minutes.

8. When the cycle is complete, remove the baking pan from the bread machine.

9. Turn the dough out onto a lightly floured surface and knead for a few minutes until the dough is elastic.

10. Place the dough into an oiled bowl and let it rise until it is double in size, about 30-40 minutes.

11. Once doubled in size, roll the dough out into a large rectangle and brush with melted butter.

12. Sprinkle with cinnamon and sugar before rolling the dough into a log shape.

13. Cut into 12 equal pieces and place into a greased baking dish.

14. Bake at 375°F for about 25 minutes.

15. Let cool before serving.

French Bread

Ingredients

-1 ½ teaspoons active dry yeast

-1 ½ cups warm water

-2 ½ cups all-purpose flour

-1 teaspoon salt

-1 tablespoon sugar

-1 tablespoon olive oil

Instructions

1. In the bread machine pan, combine the yeast, warm water, flour, salt, sugar, and olive oil in the order listed.

2. Program the bread machine to make French bread.

3. Let the bread machine knead and prepare the dough.

4. Carefully remove the dough from the pan and place it on a lightly floured surface.

5. Preheat your oven to 375 degrees F.

6. Knead the dough for several minutes before shaping it into a round loaf.

7. Place the dough on a baking sheet lined with parchment paper and set aside for 10 minutes to rest.

8. Bake the dough for 25-30 minutes, or until golden brown on top.

9. Remove from the oven, and brush with butter.

Oatmeal Bread Maker

Ingredients:

1 1/2 cups rolled oats, old-fashioned.

2 cups warmed water.

three cups bread flour

1 teaspoon granulated sugar

1 and 1/2 teaspoons salt

2 teaspoons dry active yeast

3 tablespoons softened butter or margarine.

Instructions:

1. In the bread machine, combine oats, water, bread flour, sugar, salt, active dry yeast, and butter or margarine in the order recommended by the manufacturer.

2. Close the lid and start your bread machine's dough cycle.

3. Knead and mix for 10 minutes before pressing start.

4. Let the bread machine knead the dough for another 10 minutes.

5. Pause the machine and open the lid to inspect the dough. If it's too soft, add more flour in small amounts until it's the right consistency.

6. Shut the lid and hit the start button. Allow 25 minutes for the bread machine to knead and rise.

7. Remove the dough from the bread machine after the dough cycle has finished, shape it into a

round loaf, and place it on a lightly greased baking sheet or bread pan.

Preheat the oven to 350 degrees Fahrenheit.

9. Bake the bread for 40 minutes on the center rack of the oven.

10. Remove the bread from the oven and place it on a wire rack to cool before slicing.

Whole Wheat Bread Machine

Ingredients:

-1 ½ cups of lukewarm water

-2 tablespoons of vegetable oil

-2 tablespoons of honey

-3 cups of whole wheat flour

-1 ½ teaspoons of salt

-2 teaspoons of instant dry yeast

Instructions:

1. Begin by adding the lukewarm water, oil, and honey to the bread machine.

2. Next, add the three cups of whole wheat flour into the machine.

3. Then add the salt and instant dry yeast.

4. Close the lid of the bread machine and select the "bread machine cycle".

5. Once the cycle is complete, transfer the dough to a lightly floured surface and knead it two or three times.

6. Resize the dough into a loaf and place it into a greased loaf pan.

7. Cover the pan with a kitchen towel and let it rise for about 40 minutes.

8. Preheat your oven to 375° F.

9. Gently brush the top of the dough with some oil or melted butter.

10. Allow baking for about 20 to 25 minutes or until the top is golden brown.

11. Transfer the bread to a cooling rack and allow it to cool completely.

All-purpose flour bread machine

Ingredients:

-2 cups regular flour

-1 teaspoon of salt

-2 tsp. active dry yeast

-2 tbsp. sugar or honey

-2 tbsp. vegetable oil or butter

-1 1/2 cups hot milk or water

Instructions:

1. In your bread maker pan, combine all the dry ingredients (flour, salt, yeast, and sugar or honey).

2. Pour over the dry ingredients the warm milk or water and vegetable oil or butter.

3. Close the bread maker lid and select the "dough" setting.

4. Remove the dough from the bread maker once it has finished kneading.

5. Form the dough into a loaf on a lightly floured surface.

6. Place the loaf in a greased loaf pan and set aside for an hour, or until it has doubled in size.

7. Preheat the oven to 350 degrees F.

8. Bake the bread for about 30 minutes, or until the top is golden brown.

9. Set aside for 10 minutes before slicing the bread.

Bacon bread machine

Ingredients:

- 1 ½ cups of all-purpose flour

- 1 teaspoon of baking powder

- ½ teaspoon of salt

- ¼ cup of cooked and crumbled bacon

- 3 tablespoons of vegetable oil

- ¾ cups of milk

- 1 large egg

- ¼ cup of shredded cheddar cheese

Instructions:

1. In the bread machine pan, combine all of the dry ingredients (flour, baking powder, and salt).

2. Stir in the crumbled cooked bacon.

3. Whisk together the vegetable oil, milk, and egg in a mixing bowl.

4. Place the wet ingredients in the bread machine pan.

5. Close the lid and select "dough" as the setting.

6. Once the dough has been mixed and kneaded, add the cheddar cheese.

7. Allow the pork bacon bread machine to finish its cycle. When the cycle is complete, turn the dough out onto a lightly floured surface and punch it down.

8. Shape the dough into a loaf, place it in a greased 9x5-inch loaf pan, cover it with a towel, and set it aside for an hour to rise in a warm place.

9. Bake for 30 to 35 minutes, or until golden, in a preheated 375°F oven.

10. Remove from the pan and set aside to cool before turning out and serving.

Bagels Bread Machine

Ingredients:

-6 cups all-purpose flour [with extra for dusting]

-2 tablespoons granulated sugar.

-1 tablespoon active dry yeast

-2 teaspoons salt

-2 tablespoons vegetable oil

-2 1/2 cups warm water

Instructions:

1. In the bowl of your bread machine, combine the flour, sugar, yeast, and salt. Stir in the oil and warm water until a soft dough forms.

2. Choose the dough cycle of your bread machine, and let the machine knead the dough until it is smooth and elastic.

3. When the cycle has finished, turn the dough out onto a lightly floured work surface. Separate the dough into equal parts8 and shape each piece into a smooth ball.

4. Place the balls on an ungreased baking sheet, brush with a bit of melted butter, and let rise in a warm place until doubled in size, about 1 hour.

5. Preheat oven to 375 degrees F. Bake the bagels until golden brown and they sound hollow when tapped, about 20 to 25 minutes. Serve warm.

Cranberry Bread Maker

Ingredients:

-2 eggs -1/2 cup melted butter.

1/2 cup sugar, 1/2 cup light brown sugar, 1/2 cup dried cranberries.

-1 1/2 cups of everything

-1 teaspoon baking powder -all-purpose flour

-1 tablespoon baking soda

-1/4 teaspoon ground cinnamon -1/4 teaspoon salt

-1 cup of buttermilk and -1 teaspoon of vanilla extract.

Instructions:

1. In a mixing bowl, whisk together the butter, eggs, sugar, and light brown sugar until smooth.

2. Mix in the dried cranberries to prevent them from clumping.

3. In a different bowl, sift together the flour, baking powder, baking soda, salt, and cinnamon.

4. Combine the buttermilk and vanilla extract in a third bowl.

5. Stir the dry ingredients into the butter and sugar mixture as you pour.

6. Stir in the buttermilk and vanilla extract until all the ingredients are combined.

7. Pour the batter into a greased bread machine pan and set the machine to the bread baking setting.

8. When the bread is done baking, remove it from the machine and set it aside to cool.

Garlic bread machine

Ingredients:

-1 cup all-purpose flour

-2 teaspoons baking powder

-1 teaspoon sea salt

-1/4 cup butter, softened.

-1/4 cup grated Parmesan cheese.

-1/4 teaspoon garlic powder

-2/3 cup milk

-1 teaspoon olive oil

Instructions:

1. Mix the flour, baking powder, and salt in a medium mixing bowl.

2. Stir in the softened butter and Parmesan cheese, kneading with your hands until the mixture forms a crumbly dough.

3. Whisk together the milk and olive oil in a separate bowl.

4. Knead the dough with the milk and olive oil mixture until it is soft and pliable.

5. Rest the dough for 30 minutes, covered with an inverted bowl or plastic wrap.

6. After 30 minutes, turn the dough out onto a floured surface and roll it out to 14-inch thickness.

7. Cut the dough into 3-inch-by-6-inch rectangles.

8. Arrange the dough rectangles on a greased baking sheet, sprinkle with garlic powder, and bake at 375°F for 18-20 minutes, or until golden brown.

9. Serve with butter or your preferred dip while still warm.

Honey wheat bread machine

Ingredients:

-2 tablespoons of honey

-3 cups of wheat flour

-1 teaspoon of sea salt

-1 tablespoon of dry active yeast

-1 cup of warm water

-1 teaspoon of honey

-2 tablespoons of butter

Instructions:

1. Begin by measuring out all the ingredients and combining them in a large mixing bowl ahead of time.

2. Mix the honey, wheat flour, sea salt, and active yeast in the bowl using a wooden spoon.

3. Make sure the ingredients are blended well, then slowly incorporate the warm water, stirring as you pour.

4. When the dough begins to form, knead it for 5 minutes before shaping it into a ball.

5. Place the dough ball in the bread machine pan.

6. Melt the butter and add it to the pan. Drizzle the remaining honey over the top.

7. Close the lid of the bread machine and choose the appropriate setting for honey wheat bread.

8. Allow the bread to bake and once finished, remove the bread from the pan. Allow it cool before slicing and serving.

Soft White Sandwich Bread Machine

Ingredients:

-1 cup warm water

-2 tablespoons vegetable oil

-2 tablespoons white sugar

-1 teaspoon salt

-2 tablespoons dry milk

-3 cups all-purpose flour

-2 1/2 teaspoons active dry yeast

Instructions:

1. Gather all necessary ingredients before you begin - Unbleached all-purpose flour, salt, sugar, non-fat dry milk, butter or margarine, active dry yeast, and warm water

2. Measure out sugar, salt, and dry milk, and add to a large bowl.

3. Add the yeast and flour to the bowl and stir together until combined.

4. Cut the butter or margarine into small pieces and add to the mixture.

5. Slowly pour in the warm water and mix until a soft dough forms.

6. Knead the dough for about 5 minutes until it is soft and pliable.

7. Grease a big bowl and put the dough in it.

8. Cover the bowl with plastic wrap and let it rise in a warm spot for about an hour.

9. Once the dough has doubled in size, turn it out onto a floured surface and knead it again for a few minutes.

10. Grease a loaf pan and place the dough in it.

11. Cover the pan with a damp cloth and let the dough rise until doubled in size, about 30 minutes.

12. Preheat the oven to 350 degrees Fahrenheit.

13. Place the loaf pan in the oven and bake the bread for 30 minutes.

14. Remove the loaf pan from the oven and let the bread cool for 15 minutes before serving.

Bread Machine for Greek Yogurt

Ingredients:

-1/2 cup plain Greek yogurt

-1/2 cup softened butter.

-2 eggs -1/2 cup honey

-2 cups regular flour

-1 tablespoon baking soda

-a teaspoon of baking powder

-a quarter teaspoon salt

Instructions:

1. In the bread machine pan, layer the Greek yogurt, butter, honey, and eggs in the order recommended by the manufacturer.

2. Combine the all-purpose flour, baking soda, baking powder, and salt in the bread machine pan. Stir until the ingredients are well combined.

3. Select the dough setting on the bread machine and begin the machine.

4. When the cycle is complete, remove the dough from the pan and divide it into two equal parts. Place the portions in loaf pans that have been greased.

5. Preheat the oven to 375 degrees Fahrenheit. Bake for 25-30 minutes, or until a toothpick inserted into the center of a loaf comes out clean.

6. Allow the bread to cool for 5 minutes in the pans before removing it. Place the loaves on a cooling rack to cool completely before slicing.

Calzone Dough Bread Machine

Ingredients:

- 2 ¼ cups bread flour
- 1 teaspoon active dry yeast
- 1 ½ tablespoons olive oil
- 1 tablespoon sugar
- 1 teaspoon garlic powder
- 1 teaspoon oregano
- ¾ teaspoon basil
- ¾ teaspoon salt
- ½ cup water
- ½ cup shredded cheese

Instructions:

1. Place bread flour, active dry yeast, olive oil, sugar, garlic powder, oregano, basil, and salt into the bread machine in the order suggested by your bread machine's instruction manual.

2. Slowly add the water, stirring until the ingredients in the bread machine are moist but not wet.

3. Select the dough setting on the bread machine and press the start button.

4. Add the shredded cheese for 15 minutes into the dough setting.

5. Once the dough setting is complete, remove the dough from the bread machine and shape it into the desired size and shape.

6. Place your calzone dough on a greased baking sheet and pre-bake it in the oven at 350 degrees Fahrenheit for 10-15 minutes.

7. Remove the calzone dough from the oven and let it cool.

8. Stuff and bake your calzone as desired according to your favorite recipe.

CHAPTER 3

Homemade Gluten-Free Bread Machine Recipes

Banana Coconut Bread

Banana Coconut Bread is a decadent treat that is both delicious and nutritious. This bread, which combines the natural sweetness of banana with the nutty flavor of coconut, is an excellent way to enjoy the flavors of the tropics without traveling.

This bread is moist and delicious and high in fiber and protein, so it'll keep you feeling full and satisfied with a cup of coffee.

Ingredients:

-3/4 cup coconut flour

-1/2 cup almond flour

-1/4 cup tapioca flour

-1 teaspoon baking soda

-1 teaspoon salt

-1/2 cup coconut oil

-3 large eggs

-3/4 cup honey

-1/2 cup mashed banana

-1/2 cup almond milk

-1 teaspoon vanilla extract

Preparation:

1. Grease a 9-by-5-inch loaf pan and preheat your bread machine.

2. Whisk together the coconut flour, almond flour, tapioca flour, baking soda, and salt in a medium mixing bowl.

3. Combine the coconut oil, eggs, honey, mashed banana, almond milk, and vanilla extract in a separate bowl.

4. Slowly combine the dry and wet ingredients, stirring constantly, until everything is well combined.

5. Pour the batter into the prepared loaf pan and place it in the bread machine that has been preheated.

6. Select the "gluten-free" option and press the start button.

7. Bake until the top is golden brown, and a toothpick inserted into the center comes out clean, about 30 minutes.

8. Remove the loaf from the pan with care and set aside to cool before slicing and serving.

Zucchini Bread

Zucchini Bread is a delectable and simple treat that is ideal for any occasion. It's moist and flavorful, with nutritious ingredients like freshly grated zucchini, walnuts, and cinnamon.

It's a delicious way to enjoy a delicious slice of bread with your family and friends while using up extra zucchini from your garden.

Ingredients:

-2 cups almond flour

-1/2 teaspoon baking soda

-1/2 teaspoon baking powder

-1 teaspoon salt

-1 teaspoon ground cinnamon

-1/4 cup coconut oil, melted

-1/4 cup honey

-2 large eggs

-1 cup grated zucchini

-1/2 cup almond milk

Preparation:

1. Preheat your bread machine and grease a 9 x 5-inch loaf pan.

2. Whisk together the almond flour, baking soda, baking powder, salt, and cinnamon in a medium mixing bowl.

3. Combine the coconut oil, honey, eggs, zucchini, and almond milk in a separate bowl.

4. Slowly combine the dry and wet ingredients, stirring constantly, until everything is well combined.

5. Pour the batter into the prepared loaf pan and place it in the bread machine that has been preheated.

6. Select the "gluten-free" option and press the start button.

7. Bake until the top is golden brown, and a toothpick inserted into the center comes out clean, about 30 minutes.

8. Remove the loaf from the pan with care and set aside to cool before slicing and eating.

Apple Cinnamon Bread

Apple Cinnamon Bread is a delicious and simple recipe that will please everyone. It's a delicious breakfast or dessert bread with sweet apples and fragrant cinnamon. It's a moist, sweet, and spicy treat that's sure to please your family and guests.

It's also a great way to use up any leftover apples that are too ripe to eat. So, gather your favorite apples and cinnamon and get ready to bake.

Ingredients:

-2 cups almond flour

-1 teaspoon baking soda

-1 teaspoon baking powder

-1 teaspoon ground cinnamon

-1/2 teaspoon salt

-1/4 cup coconut oil, melted

-1/4 cup honey

-2 large eggs

-1/2 cup almond milk

-1 cup chopped apples

Preparation:

1. Grease a 9-by-5-inch loaf pan and preheat your bread machine.

2. Whisk together the almond flour, baking soda, baking powder, cinnamon, and salt in a medium mixing bowl.

3. Combine the coconut oil, honey, eggs, almond milk, and chopped apples in a separate bowl.

4. Slowly combine the dry and wet ingredients, stirring constantly, until everything is well combined.

5. Pour the batter into the prepared loaf pan and place it in the bread machine that has been preheated.

6. Select the "gluten-free" option and press the start button.

7. Bake until the top is golden brown, and a toothpick inserted into the center comes out clean, about 30 minutes.

8. Remove the loaf from the pan with care and set aside to cool before slicing.

Sweet Potato Bread

Sweet Potato Bread is a filling bread made with pureed sweet potatoes.

This flavorful bread is ideal for a snack, breakfast, or dessert. It's made from all-natural ingredients and is easily gluten-free.

Sweet Potato Bread is an excellent way to get a good dose of vitamins and minerals while also enjoying a tasty treat.

It is ideal for quenching hunger while avoiding unhealthy ingredients.

Ingredients:

-2 cups almond flour

-1 teaspoon baking soda

-1 teaspoon baking powder

-1 teaspoon ground cinnamon

-1/2 teaspoon salt

-1/4 cup coconut oil, melted

-1/4 cup honey

-2 large eggs

-1/2 cup almond milk

-1 cup mashed sweet potatoes

Preparation:

1. Grease a 9-by-5-inch loaf pan and preheat your bread machine.

2. Whisk together the almond flour, baking soda, baking powder, cinnamon, and salt in a medium mixing bowl.

3. Combine the coconut oil, honey, eggs, almond milk, and mashed sweet potatoes in a separate bowl.

4. Slowly combine the dry and wet ingredients, stirring constantly, until everything is well combined.

5. Pour the batter into the prepared loaf pan and place it in the bread machine that has been preheated.

6. Select the "gluten-free" option and press the start button.

7. Bake until the top is golden brown, and a toothpick inserted into the center comes out clean, about 30 minutes.

8. Remove the loaf from the pan with care and set aside to cool before slicing.

Pumpkin Spice Bread

Pumpkin Spice Bread is a delectable and tasty fall treat. It's a moist, flavorful loaf packed with pumpkin, cinnamon, nutmeg, and other warming spices.

This bread is ideal for a relaxing evening with a cup of hot cider. It's a great snack or dessert for any autumn get-together. It's sure to please any pumpkin spice fan in your life.

Ingredients:

-2 cups almond flour

-1 teaspoon baking soda

-1 teaspoon baking powder

-1 teaspoon ground cinnamon

-1/2 teaspoon ground nutmeg

-1/2 teaspoon ground ginger

-1/4 cup coconut oil, melted

-1/4 cup honey

-2 large eggs

-1/2 cup almond milk

-1 cup pumpkin puree

Preparation:

1. Grease a 9 x 5-inch loaf pan and preheat your bread machine.

2. Whisk together the almond flour, baking soda, baking powder, cinnamon, nutmeg, and ginger in a medium mixing bowl.

3. Combine the coconut oil, honey, eggs, almond milk, and pumpkin puree in a separate bowl.

4. Slowly combine the dry and wet ingredients, stirring constantly, until everything is well combined.

5. Pour the batter into the prepared loaf pan and place it in the bread machine that has been preheated.

6. Select the "gluten-free" option and press the start button.

7. Bake until the top is golden brown, and a toothpick inserted into the center comes out clean, about 30 minutes.

8. Remove the loaf from the pan with care and set aside to cool before slicing.

Carrot Raisin Bread

Carrot Raisin Bread is a sweet and moist quick bread that's ideal for breakfast, brunch, or an afternoon snack. It's made with healthy ingredients like carrots, raisins, and cinnamon, and it's a great way to enjoy seasonal flavors all year.

It goes well with coffee, tea, or even a cup of hot cocoa because of the combination of spices and sweetness. Today, savor the distinct flavor of Carrot Raisin Bread.

Ingredients:

- 2 cups almond flour
- 1 teaspoon baking soda
- 1 teaspoon baking powder
- 1 teaspoon ground cinnamon
- 1/2 teaspoon salt
- 1/4 cup coconut oil, melted
- 1/4 cup honey
- 2 large eggs
- 1/2 cup almond milk
- 1 cup grated carrots
- 1/2 cup raisins

Preparation:

1. Preheat your bread machine and grease a 9 x 5-inch loaf pan.

2. Whisk together the almond flour, baking soda, baking powder, cinnamon, and salt in a medium mixing bowl.

3. Combine the coconut oil, honey, eggs, almond milk, grated carrots, and raisins in a separate bowl.

4. Slowly combine the dry and wet ingredients, stirring constantly, until everything is well combined.

5. Pour the batter into the prepared loaf pan and place it in the bread machine that has been preheated.

6. Select the "gluten-free" option and press the start button.

7. Bake until the top is golden brown, and a toothpick inserted into the center comes out clean, about 30 minutes.

8. Remove the loaf from the pan with care and set aside to cool before slicing and serving.

Chocolate Chip Bread

Chocolate Chip Bread is a sweet and satisfying treat that will please everyone. This tasty bread is made with all-purpose flour, sugar, butter, and semi-sweet chocolate chips.

The richness of the butter and the lightness of the flour complement the subtle sweetness of the chocolate chips. As a result, the bread is moist and flavorful, making it ideal for breakfast, a snack, or dessert. Chocolate Chip Bread is the ideal treat for any chocolate fan.

Ingredients:

-2 cups almond flour

-1 teaspoon baking soda

-1 teaspoon baking powder

-1/2 teaspoon salt

-1/4 cup coconut oil, melted

-1/4 cup honey

-2 large eggs

-1/2 cup almond milk

-1/2 cup chocolate chips

Preparation:

1. Grease a 9-by-5-inch loaf pan and preheat your bread machine.

2. Whisk together the almond flour, baking soda, baking powder, and salt in a medium mixing bowl.

3. Combine the coconut oil, honey, eggs, almond milk, and chocolate chips in a separate bowl.

4. Slowly combine the dry and wet ingredients, stirring constantly, until everything is well combined.

5. Pour the batter into the prepared loaf pan and place it in the bread machine that has been preheated.

6. Select the "gluten-free" option and press the start button.

7. Bake until the top is golden brown, and a toothpick inserted into the center comes out clean, about 30 minutes.

8. Remove the loaf from the pan with care and set aside to cool before slicing.

Walnut Bread

Walnut Bread is a tasty artisan bread with a distinct flavor. It has a crunchy and nutty flavor and is made from high-quality walnuts. It's made entirely of natural ingredients and is high in protein, fiber, and healthy fats.

Walnut bread is ideal for sandwiches, toast, or snacking. It's also a tasty side dish for any meal.

Ingredients:

-2 cups almond flour

-1 teaspoon baking soda

-1 teaspoon baking powder

-1 teaspoon ground cinnamon

-1/2 teaspoon salt

-1/4 cup coconut oil, melted

-1/4 cup honey

-2 large eggs

-1/2 cup almond milk

-1/2 cup chopped walnuts

Preparation:

1. Grease a 9 x 5-inch loaf pan and preheat your bread machine.

2. In a medium bowl, whisk together the almond flour, baking soda, baking powder, cinnamon, and salt.

3. In a separate bowl, mix the coconut oil, honey, eggs, almond milk, and chopped walnuts.

4. Slowly add the dry ingredients to the wet ingredients, stirring until everything is well combined.

5. Pour the batter into the prepared loaf pan and place it into the preheated bread machine.

6. Select the "gluten-free" setting and press start.

7. Let the bread machine do its work and bake until the top is golden brown, and a toothpick inserted into the center comes out clean.

8. Carefully remove the loaf from the pan and let cool before slicing.

Flaxseed Bread

Flaxseed bread is a type of bread made from ground flaxseeds, which are flax plant seeds. It is a high-fiber, omega-3 fatty acid, and protein-rich alternative to other types of bread.

Flaxseed bread has a nutty flavor and a chewy texture, making it an excellent sandwich and toast bread. It's also a great option for vegans and those looking for gluten-free bread.

Ingredients:

-2 cups almond flour

-1/4 cup ground flaxseed

-1 teaspoon baking soda

-1 teaspoon baking powder

-1 teaspoon ground cinnamon

-1/2 teaspoon salt

-1/4 cup coconut oil, melted

-1/4 cup honey

-2 large eggs

-1/2 cup almond milk

Preparation:

1. Preheat your bread machine and grease a 9 x 5-inch loaf pan.

2. Whisk together the almond flour, ground flaxseed, baking soda, baking powder, cinnamon, and salt in a medium mixing bowl.

3. Combine the coconut oil, honey, eggs, and almond milk in a separate bowl.

4. Slowly combine the dry and wet ingredients, stirring constantly, until everything is well combined.

5. Pour the batter into the prepared loaf pan and place it in the bread machine that has been preheated.

6. Select the "gluten-free" option and press the start button.

7. Bake until the top is golden brown, and a toothpick inserted into the center comes out clean, about 30 minutes.

8. Remove the loaf from the pan with care and set aside to cool before slicing and serving.

Blueberry Bread

Blueberry bread is a sweet, delicious bread that is ideal for breakfast, brunch, or as a snack. It's made from blueberries, sugar, and flour and comes in a variety of shapes and sizes.

Blueberry bread is a delicious way to use fresh or frozen blueberries and add flavor to any meal.

The distinct flavor of blueberries distinguishes this bread, which is sure to satisfy any sweet tooth.

Ingredients:

-2 cups almond flour

-1 teaspoon baking soda

-1 teaspoon baking powder

-1 teaspoon ground cinnamon

-1/2 teaspoon salt

-1/4 cup coconut oil, melted

-1/4 cup honey

-2 large eggs

-1/2 cup almond milk

-1 cup fresh or frozen blueberries

Preparation:

1. Grease a 9 x 5-inch loaf pan and preheat your bread machine.

2. In a medium bowl, whisk together the almond flour, baking soda, baking powder, cinnamon, and salt.

3. In a separate bowl, mix the coconut oil, honey, eggs, almond milk, and blueberries.

4. Slowly add the dry ingredients to the wet ingredients, stirring until everything is well combined.

5. Pour the batter into the prepared loaf pan and place it into the preheated bread machine.

6. Select the "gluten-free" setting and press start.

7. Let the bread machine do its work and bake until the top is golden brown, and a toothpick inserted into the center comes out clean.

8. Carefully remove the loaf from the pan and let cool before slicing and serving.

CHAPTER 4

Gluten-Free Bread Machine Tips

Choosing the Right Bread Machine

Selecting the ideal bread machine can be a tricky problem. With so many models available, deciding which one is best for you can be difficult. Before making a purchase, think about the features you require, the size and capacity, and the price.

Consider the features you require first. Do you intend to bake a large quantity of bread?

Are you looking for a machine that can make gluten-free bread?

Do you want a machine with a timer to program the baking cycle? All these factors must be considered before purchasing a machine.

Consider the size and capacity next. Some machines are small, producing only one or two loaves at a time, while others can produce four to five loaves.

If you intend to make large batches of bread, a larger machine is probably a better choice.

Finally, think about the cost. Bread machines range in price from very cheap to quite expensive. If you don't intend to use the device frequently, you might want to get a less expensive model.

If you intend to use the machine frequently, however, investing in a higher-end model may be worthwhile.

Choosing the right bread machine can be difficult. However, if you take the time to consider your needs, size and capacity, and price, you will be able to find the ideal machine for you.

Gluten-Free Bread Machine Settings

Gluten-free bread has grown in popularity in recent years as gluten intolerance, celiac disease, and other dietary restrictions have increased. While gluten-free bread can be baked in a standard oven, using a bread machine with gluten-free settings makes the process much easier.

When making gluten-free bread in a bread machine, the settings must be adjusted to account for the lack of gluten. This entails adjusting the kneading, rising, and baking times to prevent the bread from becoming too dense or dry.

Furthermore, bread machines must be equipped with a gluten-free cycle that uses a slower mix and rises time. This cycle also helps to ensure that the finished product is not too wet or gummy.

Gluten-free bread also necessitates the use of different ingredients than regular bread. Many gluten-free loaves of bread are made with a combination of flour like rice, sorghum, or buckwheat and starch like tapioca or potato starch. Furthermore, many bread machines necessitate the use of a gluten-free bread mix or gluten-free bread chine mix.

Using a bread machine with gluten-free settings can make it much easier to make delicious and nutritious gluten-free bread.

It is possible to enjoy tasty gluten-free loaves without the hassle of conventional oven baking with the right ingredients and settings.

Troubleshooting Tips

A baker wanted to create delicious gluten-free bread. Unfortunately, along the line, she encountered some difficulties while using a bread machine. She decided to take a step back and look for some troubleshooting tips after a few frustrating attempts.

1. Check your bread machine's settings. Check that you've chosen the appropriate settings for the type of bread you're making.

2. Make sure you're using the right kind of gluten-free flour. Different flours have different properties and necessitate different amounts of liquid, so choose wisely.

3. Add more flour if your dough is too wet or sticky. Add more water or oil if it's too dry or crumbly.

4. Before mixing, make sure that all of your ingredients are at room temperature.

5. Adjust the timer and/or temperature if your bread machine does not have a gluten-free setting for the best results.

6. Check the internal temperature of your finished product with a thermometer. The temperature should be at least 190 degrees Fahrenheit.

7. If your gluten-free bread is too dense or dry, try adding a little more liquid or oil.

8. Double-check that you're using the correct amount of yeast and that it's still active.

9. If your gluten-free bread is too chewy or dense, increase the amount of baking powder or baking soda used.

10. Remember that gluten-free bread requires more kneading than regular bread, so make sure to thoroughly knead it.

The baker was finally able to make delicious gluten-free bread with the help of their bread machine by following these tips.

CHAPTER 5

Doughnut Maker

This machine is perfect for making delicious doughnuts with ease and consistency.

A doughnut maker is a kitchen appliance used to make doughnuts.

It is an automated machine that mixes, shapes, and bakes doughnuts with little or no manual intervention. Doughnut makers are available in both electric and manual models.

Electric doughnut

Electric doughnut makers are typically operated with a single switch. The user adds pre-mixed dough to the hopper, sets the timer, and the doughnut maker does the rest.

Doughnuts are formed by a die-cut sheet of dough that is pushed through the machine. The dough is then automatically cooked in oil or sprayed with non-stick coating and a variety of toppings can be added to the finished product.

Manual doughnut

Manual doughnut makers are usually composed of two circular plates that are clamped together.

The user adds the pre-mixed dough in between the two plates and manually rotates the plates to shape the dough into doughnuts.

This type of doughnut maker requires more skill and effort than an electric model but is the perfect option for those who prefer the traditional hand-made doughnut.

Doughnut makers can make various doughnuts, including classic cake doughnuts, yeast-raised doughnuts, and gluten-free doughnuts. They are also a great way to make doughnuts that are filled with jam or cream.

Whether you are a professional baker or a home cook, a doughnut maker is a great purchase for anyone who loves to make doughnuts. They are easy to use, require minimal prep time, and produce delicious, high-quality doughnuts.

Classic Cake Doughnuts

Cake Doughnuts are typically available in three sizes: small (2-3 inches in diameter), medium (3-4 inches in diameter), and large (4 inches in diameter) (4–5 inches in diameter).

Ingredients

- -1 ¾ cups all-purpose flour
- -2 teaspoons baking powder
- -½ teaspoon salt
- -¼ teaspoon ground nutmeg
- -½ cup granulated sugar
- -1 large egg
- -2 tablespoons vegetable oil
- -¾ cup whole milk
- -oil for deep-frying

Instructions

1. Whisk together the flour, baking powder, salt, and nutmeg in a large bowl.

2. In a separate bowl, beat together the sugar, egg, oil, and milk until combined.

3. Gradually add the wet ingredients to the dry ingredients and mix until just combined. Do not over-mix.

4. Cover the bowl with plastic wrap and refrigerate for at least 2 hours.

5. On a lightly floured surface, roll out the dough to a ½-inch thickness.

6. Using a doughnut cutter, cut out circles of dough and transfer them to a parchment-lined baking sheet.

7. Heat oil in a deep fryer or large pot to 375°F.

8. Working in batches, fry the doughnuts for 1-2 minutes per side, or until golden brown.

9. Transfer the doughnuts to a paper towel-lined plate to drain.

10. Dust with powdered sugar or dip in your favorite glaze and serve.

Prep Time: 15 minutes.

Cook Time: 10 minutes.

Total Time: 25 minutes.

Yeast-Raised Doughnuts

Depending on the recipe, yeasted-raised doughnuts can come in a variety of sizes. Mini doughnuts are about 1 to 1.5 inches, and large doughnuts are about 3 to 4 inches.

Ingredients

-4 ½ cups all-purpose flour

-2 ¼ teaspoons active dry yeast

-1 cup milk, warmed to 110 degrees.

-½ cup granulated sugar

-1 teaspoon salt

-2 large eggs

-½ cup (1 stick) unsalted butter, melted

-Vegetable oil, for frying

Instructions

1. In a large mixing bowl, including the flour and yeast.

2. Mix the milk, sugar, salt, eggs, and melted butter in a separate bowl.

3. Combine the wet and dry ingredients and stir until a soft dough forms.

4. Knead the dough on a lightly floured board for 5 minutes.

5. Cover the dough with a clean cloth and place it in an oiled bowl. Consider one hour for the dough to rise.

6. Punch the dough down and flatten it out to a 12-inch thickness. Cut out doughnuts with a doughnut cutter.

7. Place the doughnuts on a baking sheet and set aside for 30 minutes to rise.

8. Heat 2-3 inches of oil to 375 degrees F in a large pot. Drop the doughnuts in carefully and fry for 1-2 minutes on each side, or until golden brown.

9. Remove the doughnuts from the oil and place them on a plate lined with paper towels to drain.

10. Sprinkle with powdered sugar or glaze with your preferred icing.

Preparation Time: 2 hours and 10 minutes

Time to cook: 8 minutes.

2 hours and 18 minutes total

Gluten-Free Doughnuts

Gluten-free doughnuts are available in several sizes, including mini, regular, and jumbo. Many gluten-free doughnut shops also offer custom sizes like half-sized, double-sized, and party-sized doughnuts.

Ingredients

- 2 cups gluten-free all-purpose flour

- 1/3 cup granulated sugar

- 2 teaspoons baking powder

- 1/2 teaspoon baking soda

- 1/4 teaspoon salt

- 2 large eggs

- 1/4 cup melted butter

- 1/4 cup coconut milk

- 1 teaspoon vanilla extract

Instructions

1. Heat the oven to 350°F and grease a doughnut pan lightly.

2. Whisk together the flour, sugar, baking powder, baking soda, and salt in a large mixing bowl.

3. Whisk together the eggs, melted butter, coconut milk, and vanilla extract in a separate bowl.

4. Combine the wet and dry ingredients in a mixing bowl until just combined (do not overmix).

5. Place the doughnuts in the prepared doughnut pan and bake for 10-12 minutes, or until slightly golden and springy when lightly touched.

6. Allow cooling for 5 minutes in the pan before transferring it to a wire rack to cool completely.

Time allotted: 25 minutes.

CHAPTER 6

Convection Oven

Convection oven baking uses hot air to circulate around food, cooking it faster and more smoothly than traditional ovens. Convection ovens are popular in commercial kitchens and are becoming more popular in residential kitchens.

The main distinction between a convection oven and a regular oven is that a fan circulates hot air around the food. Heat can now reach all sides of the food at the same time, resulting in faster cooking times and more even results.

This is especially useful for baking, as it ensures that cakes and cookies are thoroughly cooked without burning the edges.

Just before baking with a convection oven, keep in mind that the food will cook faster than in a regular oven. Recipes may need to be adjusted to accept responsibility for the shorter cooking times. It's also important to remember that the fan can cause food to brown faster, so reduce the temperature and bake times accordingly.

When baking with a convection oven, it is critical to use the proper cookware. Glass and metal pans are ideal for convection ovens because they allow for the best heat circulation. It is also important to place all pans on the same shelf to ensure even cooking.

Convection oven baking can help you save time and achieve more even results. Anyone can become a master of convection oven baking with a few simple changes.

CHAPTER 7

Pizza Oven

Pizza ovens are specialized ovens designed to bake pizzas. They typically use high heat and can reach temperatures up to 500°F. This ensures that the pizza crust is crispy, and the toppings are cooked perfectly.

What to Look for When Buying a Pizza Oven

There are a few key factors to consider when searching for a pizza oven.

Determine the size and shape of the oven you require first. Do you intend to make individual-sized pizzas or large family-style pizzas? Is it more convenient to have a countertop oven or a large floor model in a commercial kitchen? Knowing the size and shape you require will aid in narrowing your search.

Next, consider the fuel you intend to use. The most common ovens are electric, but gas and wood-fired ovens provide a more authentic flavor. Electric ovens are usually less expensive, whereas gas and wood-fired ovens are more expensive.

Take note of the oven's temperature range as well. Most electric ovens can reach temperatures of 500°F or higher, while gas and wood-fired ovens can reach temperatures of 800°F or higher. The higher the temperature range, the faster and more evenly the oven will cook pizzas.

Finally, think about any extra features that might be useful. Some ovens have adjustable shelves or rotating racks that can help you cook large pizzas evenly. Furthermore, some ovens include a built-in timer, which can help prevent pizzas from burning.

By taking these factors into account, you can ensure that you get the best pizza oven for your needs.

Types of Pizza Ovens

1. **Wood-Fired Pizza Ovens**: These are traditional ovens that run on wood. They typically reach high temperatures, giving the pizza a smoky flavor.

2. **Gas Pizza Ovens**: These ovens are powered by natural gas or propane. They are typically more efficient and have better temperature control than wood-fired ovens.

3. **Electric Pizza Ovens**: These ovens run on electricity and are typically the most convenient and cost-effective option. They are simple to use and maintain, and they can quickly reach high temperatures.

4. **Conveyor Pizza Ovens**: These ovens move the pizza from one end of the oven to the other using a

conveyor belt. They are ideal for large-scale operations and can produce many pizzas at once.

5. **Brick Ovens**: These ovens use a combination of wood and gas as fuel and are frequently made of brick or stone. They are well-known for their crisp, flavorful pizza.

Benefits of Owning a Pizza Oven

1. **Greater Efficiency**: Pizza ovens heat up quickly and retain heat for a longer period, allowing you to cook multiple pizzas in a short period of time. This makes them ideal for crowded restaurants or large gatherings.

2. **Versatility**: Pizza ovens can bake bread, roast meats, and even make desserts in addition to pizza.

3. **Improved Flavor**: Pizza ovens create a distinct atmosphere that contributes to better-tasting pizza. The high heat speeds up the cooking process, which seals in the flavor.

4. **Low Maintenance**: Pizza ovens don't require much upkeep. They can be cleaned with a damp cloth and do not require calibration, as do other ovens.

5. **Cost Savings**: Investing in a pizza oven can save you money in the long run because it is more efficient than a standard oven and can also be used to cook other foods.

6. **Fun**: Pizza ovens are a great way to make cooking more enjoyable. Invite friends and family over to help you make homemade pizza or throw an outdoor pizza party.

7. **Quality**: A pizza oven produces much better pizza than a regular oven. A pizza oven generates much hotter heat than a regular oven and can cook a pizza much faster, resulting in a perfectly cooked pizza with a crisp, flavorful crust.

How to Care for a Pizza Oven

1. Keep the oven clean on a regular basis. Make a point of cleaning out any debris or grease that has

accumulated inside the oven. Remove any build-up that has occurred with a wire brush and a vacuum cleaner.

2. Ensure adequate ventilation. If your pizza oven does not receive adequate air circulation, temperature regulation issues may arise. When not in use, leave the oven door open and keep the vents clean.

3. Check the temperature on a regular basis. Check the thermometer on a regular basis to ensure that the oven is at the proper temperature. Adjust the thermostat if it is too hot or too cold.

4. Use the proper fuel. Use the appropriate fuel for your pizza oven. Wood is the traditional fuel source, but depending on the type of oven, you can also use charcoal or propane.

5. Keep the oven away from the elements. If your pizza oven is outside, keep it covered during inclement weather. This will shield it from rain, snow, and other elements.

6. Use pizza stones always. Pizza stones aid in the even distribution of heat and ensure that your pizzas come out perfectly. When cooking, make sure to use them.

Safety Tips for Using a Pizza Oven

1. When handling hot pizza ovens and pizza pans, always wear heat-resistant gloves and oven mitts.

2. Position the oven on a level, stable surface.

3. Ensure that the area around the oven is well-ventilated and free of flammable materials.

4. Preheat the oven before using it.

5. Preheat the pizza pan before adding the pizza.

6. Place and remove the pizza from the oven using a pizza peel or a long-handled utensil.

7. Check the oven temperature on a regular basis to ensure it is at the proper temperature.

8. When you're finished, turn off the oven and let it cool before cleaning it.

9. Never leave the oven running unattended.

10. Clean the oven on a regular basis to prevent food debris build-up.

Quick Recipes for Making Pizza in a Pizza Oven

1. Preheat the oven to 500°F (260°C).

2. Flour your pizza peel and stretch out your pizza dough.

3. Add desired sauces, cheeses, and toppings to your pizza dough.

4. Carefully slide the pizza onto the oven's preheated stone.

5. Bake for 8-10 minutes until the crust is golden brown and the cheese has melted.

6. Using a pizza peel, remove the cooked pizza from the oven and set aside for a few minutes before slicing.

Troubleshooting Common Pizza Oven Issues

Pizza ovens are a popular piece of restaurant equipment, but they can be finicky and cause a lot of problems if not properly maintained. Certainly, there are some common problems that can be easily identified and resolved.

1. **Thermostat Failure**: Pizza ovens require a specific temperature in order to properly bake the pizza. The thermostat may fail if the oven does not reach the required temperature.

To test this, use an oven thermometer to measure the temperature of the oven. If the oven is not reaching the desired temperature, the thermostat may need to be replaced.

2. **Ignition Problems**: The pizza oven may not light due to an ignition problem. Check the ignitor in the oven to ensure it is working properly. Otherwise, it may need to be replaced.

3. **Blocked Vents**: Pizza ovens require proper ventilation to function properly. If the vents are blocked, the oven will overheat, making it difficult for the pizza to cook properly. Examine the vents for any obstructions and remove them if necessary.

4. **Dirty Oven**: Over time, pizza ovens can become clogged with grease and food particles. This can cause the oven to overheat, resulting in an unevenly cooked pizza. Use an oven-cleaning solution and a scrub brush to remove any built-up residue from the oven.

Common pizza oven problems can be resolved to keep your restaurant running smoothly. Any of the issues listed above can be resolved quickly with a little time and effort.

CHAPTER 8

Rotisserie Oven

A rotisserie oven is a specialized oven that uses rotating spits to cook food. The rotating spits ensure that the food is cooked evenly and consistently over time. Rotisserie ovens are great for roasting large cuts of meat, such as whole chickens or turkeys.

Types Of Rotisserie Ovens

1. Countertop Rotisserie Ovens

2. Built-in Rotisserie Ovens

3. Commercial Rotisserie Ovens

4. Outdoor Rotisserie Ovens

5. Electric Rotisserie Ovens

6. Convection Rotisserie Ovens.

Gluten-Free Recipes to Make with a Rotisserie Oven.

Rotisserie Baked Sweet Potato Fries: Preheat your rotisserie oven to 375°F. Cut two large, sweet potatoes into quarter-inch slices.

Season with sea salt, black pepper, garlic powder, and paprika in a large mixing bowl. Sprinkle with olive oil and toss to evenly coat. Bake for 30-35 minutes, or until golden brown and crispy, on a rotisserie pan.

Rotisserie Roasted Vegetables: Heat the rotisserie oven to 375°F. Cut your favorite vegetables (such as bell peppers, squash, zucchini, mushrooms, onions, and so on) into 1-inch chunks.

Season with sea salt, black pepper, garlic powder, and rosemary in a large mixing bowl. Sprinkle with olive oil and toss to evenly coat. Bake for 15-20 minutes, stirring halfway through, on a rotisserie pan.

Rotisserie Roasted Potatoes: Heat the rotisserie oven to 375°F. Cut two large potatoes into quarter-inch thick slices. Season with sea salt, black pepper, garlic powder, and rosemary in a large mixing bowl. Sprinkle with olive oil and toss to evenly coat.

Bake for 30-35 minutes, stirring halfway through, on a rotisserie pan.

Rotisserie Grilled Cheese Sandwiches: Preheat the rotisserie oven to 375°F for the Rotisserie Grilled Cheese Sandwiches. On one side of two slices of gluten-free bread, spread butter. Place a rotisserie pan with the butter side down.

Top with your preferred cheese and the remaining slices of bread, butter-side up. Bake for 10-12 minutes, or until the cheese has melted and the bread has turned golden brown.

Rotisserie Stuffed Peppers: Heat the rotisserie oven to 375°F. Remove the seeds and membranes from four bell peppers and place them on a rotisserie pan. Combine cooked quinoa, cooked black beans, fresh tomatoes, red onion, garlic, and fresh cilantro in a mixing bowl. Season with cumin, black pepper, and sea salt.

Stuff each pepper half with the quinoa mixture and top with your favorite cheese. Bake the peppers for 15-20 minutes, or until tender.

Rotisserie Roasted Chicken: Heat the rotisserie oven to 375°F. Season a whole chicken with sea salt, black pepper, garlic powder, and paprika, and place it on the rotisserie. 1 hour and 15 minutes, or until the internal temperature reaches 165°F. Leave it for a 5-minute before serving.

Rotisserie Jerk Chicken: Preheat your rotisserie oven to 375°F. Set up a rotisserie with a whole chicken. In a mixing bowl, combine olive oil, apple cider vinegar, onion powder, garlic powder, allspice, ground ginger, cayenne pepper, and thyme. Cook for 1 hour and 15 minutes until the internal temperature reaches 165 degrees F. Leave it for a 5-minute before serving.

Rotisserie Grilled Pineapple: Preheat the rotisserie oven to 375°F for the grilled pineapple. Place a pineapple on a rotisserie pan and cut it into 1-inch-thick slices.

Pour with honey and sprinkle with cinnamon. Bake the pineapple for 20-25 minutes, or until golden brown and caramelized.

Buffalo Rotisserie Cauliflower: Preheat the rotisserie oven to 375°F. Place one head of cauliflower in florets on a rotisserie pan. In a mixing bowl, combine the olive oil, hot sauce, garlic powder, and onion powder.

Sprinkle the mixture over the cauliflower and bake for 15-20 minutes, or until tender. Dress with ranch or blue cheese dressing and serve.

Rotisserie Baked Apples: Preheat the rotisserie oven to 375°F. Place four apples on a rotisserie pan and cut them into 1-inch-thick slices. Sprinkle honey over the top and sprinkle with cinnamon. Bake the apples for 20-25 minutes, or until golden brown and tender. Serve with an ice cream scoop.

Health Benefits

Increased Nutrient Intake: Eating gluten-free recipes made with a rotisserie oven can help gluten-free eaters increase their nutrient intake. Because they use less oil and fat, foods cooked in a rotisserie oven are generally healthier than deep-fried or pan-fried foods.

This means that gluten-free eaters can enjoy a wide range of recipes without having to worry about extra fat and calories.

Improved Digestive Health: Rotisserie cooking aids in the breakdown of proteins and carbohydrates, making the food easier to digest. This is especially beneficial for those who have gluten intolerance or celiac disease, as gluten-containing products can irritate their digestive systems.

Reduced Risk of Foodborne Illness: Because of its high temperatures and low moisture content, rotisserie cooking is known to reduce the risk of foodborne illness.

This makes it an excellent cooking method for those with weakened immune systems or who are predisposed to food-borne illnesses.

Reduced Cross-Contamination Risk: Rotisserie ovens typically cook only one type of food at a time. This reduces the risk of cross-contamination, which is important for people who are gluten sensitive or allergic.

Versatility: Rotisserie ovens can be used to prepare a wide range of dishes, including roasted vegetables, grilled meats, and more. This makes it an excellent choice for anyone looking to prepare healthy, delicious gluten-free recipes.

Convenience: Rotisserie ovens are simple to use and require little clean-ups, making them an ideal choice for busy households. They also take less time to prepare than other cooking methods, which can save time and energy.

Reduced Cost: Rotisserie ovens are reasonably priced and can be used to prepare a wide range of gluten-free recipes.

This makes them an excellent choice for those on a tight budget who want to eat a healthy, gluten-free meal.

Eating gluten-free recipes made with a rotisserie oven can be a delicious way to enjoy nutritious meals without sacrificing taste, texture, or health benefits.

Issues And Solutions - Bread Creators

1. Dough not mixing properly - This can be caused by over-measuring ingredients, not adding enough liquid, or using an overly aggressive setting for the type of dough being mixed. Check the measurements to ensure they are precise, add a bit

more liquid, and try a less aggressive setting to fix this.

2. Dough not rising - This can be caused by using too little yeast or not allowing enough time for the dough to rise. To correct this, use the correct amount of yeast and allow the dough to rise for a longer period.

3. Excessive kneading noise - This can be caused by a loose blade or a worn-out belt. Check the blade and belt for wear and replace them if necessary.

Solutions:

1. Use a timer - Using a timer can help ensure that the machine does not overwork itself.

2. Check the ingredients - Before adding the ingredients to the bread machine, double-check the ingredients and measurements.

3. Clean the machine on a regular basis - Cleaning the machine on a regular basis will help keep it running smoothly and reduce the likelihood of problems occurring.

4. Use the proper settings - Different types of dough necessitate different temperatures. Choose the appropriate setting for the type of dough being mixed.

5. Read the manual - Reading the manual can help ensure that the machine is used correctly and identify any potential problems.

6. Check the dough - After mixing, check the dough to make sure it's the right consistency. This will aid in identifying any potential issues before baking.

7. Troubleshoot - If problems arise, consult the manual or contact the manufacturer.

8. Allow the machine to cool - Allow the machine to completely cool before storing or reusing it.

9. Properly store the machine - When not in use, keep the machine in a dry, cool place.

10. Replace parts as needed - Parts can wear out and need to be replaced over time. Replacing these

parts can help extend the life of the machine and ensure proper operation.

11. Use caution when handling hot parts - To avoid burns, use an oven mitt or other protective gear when handling hot parts.

12. Follow safety guidelines - When using the bread machine, always follow the manufacturer's safety guidelines.

13. Use the correct ingredients - For the best results, use the ingredients listed in the recipe.

14. Use the correct pans - Use the correct pan for the recipe and the size of the bread machine.

15. Use caution when removing the bread - Use caution when removing the bread from the machine to avoid burns from the hot pan.

16. Properly store bread - After it has cooled, store it in an airtight container to keep it fresh.

17. Use a thermometer - To ensure that the bread is cooked to the desired temperature, use a thermometer.

18. Use a bread knife - Slice the bread with a bread knife. This will help to keep the bread from being crushed.

19. Allow the machine to cool completely before storing it - Allow the machine to cool completely before storing it.

20. Unplug the machine - When not in use, always unplug the bread machine.

These are some of the most common bread machine problems and solutions. Following these guidelines can help to ensure that your bread machine operates properly and efficiently.

CONCLUSION

Gluten, a protein found in wheat, barley, and rye, has been linked to a variety of serious health issues in people who are gluten intolerant. Celiac disease is the most severe form of gluten intolerance and can damage the small intestine for life.

Gluten is also linked to gluten ataxia, dermatitis herpetiformis, and non-celiac gluten sensitivity. Gluten intolerance can cause digestive discomfort, fatigue, headaches, joint pain, and skin rashes. Gluten-intolerant people should avoid all products containing wheat, barley, or rye.

Fortunately, many gluten-free products are now available to help people with gluten intolerance maintain a healthy diet. However, just because a product is labelled "gluten-free," it does not always mean it is free of all gluten-containing ingredients. As a result, it is critical to carefully read the labels of all food products to ensure that they are truly gluten-free.

People with gluten intolerance may need to take supplements in addition to following a gluten-free diet to ensure that they are getting the nutrients they require. It is critical to consult with a healthcare professional about the best supplements for your specific needs.

Gluten-intolerant people can live healthy and active lives if they make appropriate dietary and lifestyle changes.

The goal of this cookbook has been to show you how to use your bread machine to make delicious gluten-free bread and other baked goods.

You have the assurance that the recipes in this cookbook are safe and dependable, and that you can rely on the results. You can also be confident that the bread you make will be gluten-free, allowing you to offer your family a healthy and delicious alternative to regular bread.

This cookbook has given you the tools you need to make gluten-free bread that is as good as, if not better than, traditional bread. You can now confidently make bread that your family and friends will enjoy.

With this cookbook in hand, you can now make delectable gluten-free bread for your family that you can be proud of.

Made in the USA
Columbia, SC
27 February 2023

13054881R00080